H
GI
PUNNING

A LITTLE BOOK OF JOKES

compiled by
Scott Montgomery

Acorn Books
www.acornbooks.co.uk

Hit the Ground Punning

Published in 2023 by
Acorn Books
acornbooks.uk

Hit the Ground Punning

Here Come the Puns...

*I keep up with 'Songs of Praise'. But
I don't watch it religiously!*

*I need help with my addiction to buying
batteries. Just heading to my first AA Meeting.*

I sometimes think I play Tetris just to fit in.

*I also got into a Twitter argument
about Tetris – and got blocked.*

*My partner lovingly looks after a
lighthouse. She's a keeper.*

*I'm obsessed with emptying my wheelie
bin. Just putting that out there.*

*My mum always said, 'There are no
wrong answers here.' Shame about
her job at the exams board.*

*My laptop is always covered in crumbs.
I keep refreshing my cookies.*

INTERROGATION. That's a big ask.

My joke about Dorian Gray? That never gets old.

In the pub, I like to start off with a heavy-duty sander. Helps take the edge off.

My brother-in-law likes to dress as a Batman villain. He's the Bane of my life.

*I saw that new
Caped Crusader film.
'Batman Forever?'
No, it was about three hours.*

My work colleague likes to cause trouble for Batman. He's the office Joker.

Huh. So what if I live in the UK's huffiest county? – Stropshire.

My new telly has a collar and tie. It's a smart TV.

Things have been tough in the balloon industry. I was recently let go.

I went on a double date with some Sudoku enthusiasts. Think I was there to make up the numbers.

I've got an idea for a sit-com set in a garage/ carwash – 'Only Fuels and Hoses'.

*Déja vu jokes? People are
developing heard immunity.*

*Liam Neeson likes to do the cooking. He
has a very particular set of skillets.*

*I joined that new dating site for people in
charge of monkeys – Orgn Grindrr.*

*I've also downloaded a dating app
for baristas – Bean Grindrr.*

*The barista keeps stamping on my
coffee. Now it's a flat white.*

*I need an anecdote about a clumsy
barista. Spill the beans.*

*There was trouble at work the other day
and a man was sacked.
'He left under a cloud?'
No, security escorted him to the front door.*

*A killer used a large book of calculus and
trigonometry on his victims. Police have
described him as a 'maths murderer'.*

*I'm keen to do another joke about
trigonometry but I need a new angle.*

The old folks' home is being turned into an Indian restaurant. At least I'll still see my naan.

Have you heard of that former politician who cries all the time? Ed Bawls.

The future of law enforcement is part fisherman, part policeman – Rowboat Cop.

I've become accustomed to using certain items in my toolkit. I know the drill.

At the age of fifty, I've reached a point in my life where I have feelings of remorse and anxiety about never having delivered any babies. I think it's a midwife crisis.

I just found out I was adopted by Queen Nefertiti. I always was a bit of a Mummy's boy.

There is an English connection to Egyptian ancient wonders. Cockney builders worked on the Great Pyramid of Geezer.

I mislaid the synopsis to my novel, 'Allotment'. I lost the plot.

I recommend staying at the Yoga Hotel. They bend over backwards to accommodate you.

The butcher lost no time in telling me how he nearly dropped his novel manuscript at work. He didn't mince his words.

Traffic police advise that a lorry-load of magnets has broken down on the motorway. It's a bit of a sticking point.

My experimental artificial eye is faulty. It's on the blink.

There have been lots of sniffles, coughs and sore throats on TikTok and Insta. It's down to a new Internet Influenza.

I think I'll tidy up the alphabet. I'll start with a D-clutter.

I've moved my desk out into the garden as I'm still working from gnome.

I was annoyed to discover I had been cloned. I was beside myself.

I can't tell you how delighted I was to get a job testing beds - made up.

Before any holidays, I like to cover myself in salt, pepper and herbs. I'm a seasoned traveller.

*I have a recurring bad dream where
I'm a high-ranking official in municipal
government – it's a bit of a mayor.*

*My pet swallowed part of the old vacuum
cleaner. I've let the bag out of the cat.*

*In winter I wear clothes made from onions.
You can never have too many layers.*

*I tried to take over a board games
company but its stocks had plummeted
due to faulty products. No dice.*

*My wife and I got lost in the Vatican, stumbled
down the Spanish Steps and fell in the
Trevi Fountain – hapless Rome antics.*

Dot. John Thaw. Dash. This pun is in Morse Code.

*The teacher at my ceramics class swears
a lot. She's really pottery-mouthed.*

*How do you scan something for a
pirate? Use a Q-Aaarrr code.*

*I've deposited an umbrella in the
bank. Something for a rainy day.*

I've been stocking up on food from the stationers' shop. I'm on a staple diet.

My new Porsche is full of Minestrone, clam chowder and Gazpacho. It's souped up.

I've hired a vehicle bodyshop specialist to give my car a sporty new look – spoiler alert.

Another person has come up with a pun about mending socks. Darn.

Police were called to an incident at a life drawing class. Details are sketchy.

As a teenager I was obsessed with the weapons on Star Trek. It was just a phaser I was going through.

Health & safety is important at the burlesque club. They always do a risqué assessment.

Why did I buy that house out of The Exorcist? I don't know what possessed me.

A farmer turned comedian did an hour-long routine about his cow. He was milking it a bit.

An Amazon driver became a stand-up comedian.
He couldn't gain entry to the venue so he
did his act from inside the wheelie bin.

His delivery was pretty good but then he
pestered people for reviews afterwards.

An electrician also became a
stand-up comedian. He lit up the circuit.

My favourite 1970s toy was a soldier doll who
also worked at Sotheby's – Auction Man.

I'm starting my own plumbing services'
review website – Dripadvisor.

I'm a fan of that singer who communicates
with spirits – Séancé.

I like to talk to ghostly spirits in the West
of Scotland – using a Weegie board.

I'm really into that new band,
Industrial Ventilation – big fan.

I'm retiring from investigating the
paranormal. I've given up the ghost.

Sid James, Hattie Jacques and Kenneth Williams
were not allowed on a flight – even as Carry Ons.

1977 told me to get stuffed, 2001 called
me a loser and 2023 said I was an old
git. The years haven't been kind.

I've got a new Brain-GPS – stops
my mind wandering.

The local mausoleum is getting into
finance – using crypt-ocurrency.

My guitar-playing makes people cry.
Must be that new wah-wah pedal.

I find dieting surprisingly easy.
'A piece of cake?'
No, thanks. I just said I was on a diet.

I wish my hairdresser friend wouldn't
serve lunch in her salon. We had
Sunday roast with all the trimmings.

My GP seemed reluctant to tell me if I
had eczema, psoriasis or scabies. He
didn't want to make a rash decision.

*There was some kind of scandal at the
Annual General Meeting of Cleaners –
but it was swept under the carpet.*

*I love that Oasis song about fishing
– Don't Look Back in Angler.*

*People warned me there was no future in
using semaphore. My career is flagging.*

*My new job as a foreign correspondent?
Nothing to write home about.*

*I suppose working on the ghost train
isn't a bad way to 'eek' out a living.*

*If I want to succeed in the ointment industry
I will have to apply myself daily.*

*In my new job as a roadie, I'm
happy to take on feedback.*

*I rang up a builder and asked for a quote. He
said, 'To be or not to be. That is the question.'*

*Two strangers got together at the
supermarket checkout. They became an
unexpected item in the bagging area.*

Another couple met at a funfair
coconut shy. They really hit it off.

I'm looking online for
something that will help me
sleep in short bursts.
'Have you tried downloading a nap?'

Respect to my fellow town criers – big shout-out.

I'm a fan of that 80s action movie where Bruce
Willis plays Rugby League – Try Hard.

There has been a spate of thefts involving
keyboard instruments from churches.
Police are calling it organised crime.

What's better – propane or kerosene?
Hydrogen or methane? Wood or charcoal?
So many burning questions.

Dunno why there was such a fuss
about me hiring a comedian during
afternoon tea. What a brew ha ha.

Prince Charles had doubts about becoming
King. He nearly took a reign check.

*I'm trying to call the laundry but the
number keeps wringing out.*

*I'm quitting my job in the funeral parlour.
Too many people are giving me grief.*

*I went into the pub
and asked for an entendre.
The barman said, 'Here's a large one.'
I replied, 'I didn't ask for a double.'*

*I went to
Cambridge University in......
But that was my gap year.*

*I've given up going on protest marches.
I've handed in my notice.*

*I was once in a band called Bed Linen.
We mainly followed sheet music.*

*We changed our name to The Duvets
as we specialised in covers.*

*I thought I did very well in putting a
cradle together – rocked it.*

*I've been given responsibility for a
wrecking ball – smashed it.*

Then I did some part-time work at
the recycling plant – crushed it.

Tyre prices are going up. Must be inflation.

NASA is complaining of rising costs. Their
maintenance bills are rocketing.

NASA has also hired a think-tank of stoners
to develop their latest study into the creation
of the universe – The Big Bong Theory.

To secure the rights to a new book,
'The History of the Microwave Oven' -
publishers entered into a b-ding war.

Classic vaudeville double act Laurel and
Hardy split up due to music hall differences.

Whenever I see the suitcase carousel at
the airport I cry. It's emotional baggage.

Two snow ploughs nearly ended up in a head-
on collision. That was a gritty drama.

I'm not really a fan of musicals. But I don't
like to make a big song and dance about it.

This morning I woke to the sound of the birds tweeting. Wish they'd put their mobiles on silent.

Little Bo Peep went into a garage, complaining of a headache. The mechanic said, 'Okay, I'll look under the bonnet.'

I went to see that new comedian, Polly Hedron – very edgy.

Working behind a bar has skincare benefits. It's good for the pours.

There's a new rom-com about a man who compiles encyclopaedias. Love Factually.

Hugh Grant is attached but wants a Commonwealth Games theme. Love Archery.

I'm not sure of its target audience but the idea has set hearts a-quiver.

Now the producers have decided to turn it into a vampire film. Love Artery.

Police have infiltrated a large group of shepherds. They were informed it was full of crooks.

There was a medical emergency when a man, whose basic grammar was terrible, lapsed into a comma.

I placed a bowl over my head and cut my hair before heading to the Scottish capital. I love the Edinburgh Fringe.

My wife must be keen on the fresh fruit business. She keeps saying I should grow a pear.

The baker was unsure about retirement – but was also loaf to continue.

Jokes about chocolate and biscuits? They're unsavoury.

Jokes about Satan? They're un-savioury.

Did you hear about the sewing machinist turned comedian? She has lots of fresh material.

Constantly having to pay fees to cross road bridges – it's taken a toll on me.

*What's an Arabic demon's favourite
tipple? Djinn & tonic.*

*Mum and dad are protective of their
favourite brand of chocolate bar –
they're Guardians of the Galaxy.*

*After a regeneration, Doctor Who looked in
the mirror and said, 'It's not really me.'*

*A bunch of artists gathered round their shared
workspace to discuss the previous nights' reality
TV show finale. It was a watercolour moment.*

*I fell asleep during Monopoly and dreamt
I was climbing the walls of a Mayfair
hotel – at the top of my game.*

*After the Prince Andrew scandal, the
late Queen considered laser surgery
for unwanted heir removal.*

*I saw two giants playing poker.
It was kind of a big deal.*

*My anecdote about the definition of the
word 'mandatory'? You had to be there.*

I heard your pet has super-strength. What's the matter – cat got your tonne?

I'm so angry at my high blood pressure reading. I think I have a temper-ature.

I was so nervous about my interview to become a baker, I even forgot what bread was made of – doh!

Sir Isaac Newton? Apple? Tree? Not sure I understand the gravity of the situation.

I'm really missing my dentist. Abscess makes the heart grow fonder.

I'm not sure if my friendship with a mate can survive an upcoming stag weekend.
'Acid test?'
Yes, but his name's Dave. Not Sid.

I still say the Beatles were a hard act to follow. They had really good personal security.

GOING ONCE, GOING TWICE, GOING THREE TIMES! Auctions speak louder than words.

Can I have some
free range eggs, please?
'No, you can pay for them like everyone else.'

So you were telling me how you
were stranded on a desert island?
'Sorry, I was miles away.'

I've come up with a joke
about 1980s post-punk
band Orange Juice.
Rip it up and start again?'
You might at least let me read it out first.

I've also got a pun about Jarvis Cocker
delivering religious sermons.
'Pulpit?'
That one too? I'm not doing well
with these music gags.

I've spent a long time hitting the numbers 2, 4
and 6 with a hammer. One day I'll break even.

I've spent the last few years writing a novel called
'Sandwiches'. That's my bread and butter.

After a sunbed mishap, I've given
up on getting a tan for now.
'On the back burner?'
Yeah, my front got a bit too.

*I was reluctant to get back into archaeology
as I felt I was going over old ground.*

*Granddad served with the RAF during the war but
didn't get on well with his Commanding Officer.
'Took a lot of flak?'
No, he was ground crew, I think.*

*On the way to hospital, Grandad stopped for some
sausage for lunch. He took a turn for the wurst.*

*Where is a snide Pharaoh buried?
In a sarky-ophagus.*

*I wish dad hadn't married that lawyer. My new
step-mum couldn't wait to get her clause in him.*

*We went to a nice restaurant in South London.
'Clapham?'
Well, the meat was good but it didn't
deserve a round of applause.*

*It's my Entomology exam today so I've
been doing some last-minute swatting.*

*I didn't enjoy that new Sweeney
Todd-themed Italian restaurant.
'Penny Dreadful?'
Yes, and the fusilli wasn't much better.*

I expect to be retired by age 67 and enjoying myself on the swings. At a push.

I've done the majority of my research on the behaviour of a wild species native to Africa.
'The lion's share?'
Possibly but they're usually quite possessive.

In Las Vegas I went to an exotic animals-themed casino. Spent ages at the sloth machines.

So I'm guessing you already know the first rule of Presumption Club?

I met a man who worked
in the oil industry.
'Crude?'
No, refined.

Where's the best place to find pictures of David Hasselhoff running along a beach?
'Try eBaywatch.'

A flan? Sounds like a plan.

Where do pantomime villains go for a sunshine holiday?
The Bwa-ha-ha-mas.

How many times do have to tell you to keep up
with your hieroglyphics studies?
'Okay, I get the picture.'

That new zombie nightclub? I
wouldn't be seen dead in there.

My ex-partner used to make lots of
demands while under the influence of
cannabis. She was high maintenance.

At a cosplay event I saw Harley Quinn chatting
up the Flash. She was trying to pull a fast one.

I want to fit some yoga into my day, but my
work schedule means I'm not very flexible.

I'm going to buy some LPs on eBay.
'Vinyl offer?'
Well, the bidding hasn't even opened yet.

I'm grateful to my wife for her support
during my addiction to listening to
classical music. She's got my Bach.

I went to a Morrissey gig in Torquay and
Devon Knows I'm Miserable Now.

21

In my weekend guise of DJ Potato, my audiences always enjoy a good mash-up.

Now I'm dropping a playlist as DJ Fruit Preserves. That's my jam.

I saw a zombie at the piano. He was playing by ear.

That new gold-plated toilet just cost me six months' wages. 'Flush?' I certainly hope it does at that price.

My nan and her friends like to put on gold chains and signet rings and go for a night out down the Blingo.

My neighbour is obsessive about maintaining his garden decking but now he's varnished off the face of the Earth.

I invited a plastic surgeon to see my backyard after someone said my garden needed a facelift.

The SAS just did a great Edinburgh Fringe show. Stormed it.

The comedy club didn't have any half-man/half-horse acts. A shame as I'm a huge satyr fan.

At the ice-cream parlour I asked for a quadruple knickerbocker glory. The waitress said, 'That's a tall order.'

When I was a teenager
I loved Ska fashion.
'Pork pie hat?'
No, it was made of felt, I think.

How does the leader of the Roman Catholic Church conduct financial business? Using Papal.

That cannibal is extremely persistent. A-gnaw-ing.

Someone smashed up my vintage Aretha Franklin, Otis Reading and Stevie Wonder records. Soul-destroying.

A jellyfish was put on trial. That won't stand up in court.

James Bond was on a wheat-free mission but had to check his Dietary requirements Another Day.

I love going to restaurants where I can hardly eat anything on the menu. I'm a gluten for punishment.

A cowboy came into my
car showroom and said, ''Owdy?'
I replied, 'Sorry, sir. We only sell BMWs here.'

In the operating theatre the surgical
table was uncomfortable, the life support
machine was noisy and the lights were
too bright. My condition was critical.

Then the medical staff brought in some
hay and a manger and now I'm stable.

Anyone know Ross, Rachel, Phoebe, Joey,
Chandler and Monica? Asking for a Friend.

Could someone please order me a brand
of throat lozenges from Lancashire?
Asking for a Fisherman's Friend.

I was accidentally locked in overnight
at Fort Knox. Regarding compensation,
it was worth my wait in gold.

Doctor Jekyll? He's his own worst enemy.

A heatwave ruined Don McLean's
road-trip to Rome. Drove his Chevy to
the Trevi but the Trevi was dry.

*I've got a hot wife. She tells me
it's the menopause.*

*I'll have Jagger, Hucknall and
Fleetwood. I love Pick & Micks.*

Talking of Pick & Mix - Sweeeeeet.

*There's a job going at the marionette factory.
My dad's gonna pull a few strings.*

*There was a bunch of WAGs at the golf
course – playing pitch and pout.*

*I saw some ladies' hairdressers on a night
out at the all-you-can-eat bouffant.*

Where do cultured cats go? To the mew-seum.

*Regarding two-wheeled, horse-drawn
carriages - Charioty Always Begins at Rome.*

*Me [At the GP]: Can you name
the first James Bond film?
Doctor: No.*

*I need another word for a red, tasselled
Moroccan hat. I'll look it up in a fez-aurus.*

My Scottish pal could do with some
moral support in his job at the mortuary.
A friend in need is a friend in deid.

Bat. That's half the Battle.

While in prison I took up yoga. It
was a two-year stretch.

I'm unpopular in the cheese-making
industry. Persona non-grater.

My wife attached a spring to either leg
and walked down the stairs. She did say
she would wear something slinky.

I was concerned about continually imagining I was
hurtling down a Yorkshire hill in an iron bath. But
my GP assures me I am fully Compo mentis.

I'm studying for a degree.
'Open University?'
No, the janitors do that each morning.

A comedian did a show for a room full
of cage-fighters. Tough crowd.

James Bond skips his cooked breakfast
most mornings. No Time to Fry.

Not sure how to conduct yourself at a graffiti art exhibition? Read the room.

I love an 80s mullet hairdo. That's the long and the short of it.

I had problems with my heating so I checked the boiler cupboard. Biggles was in there holding a torch. At least the pilot light was on.

The people who stole my 6-foot mirror need to take a long hard look at themselves.

I've eaten a lamp. Just a light lunch.

My new talking jigsaw is my soulmate. It said, 'You complete me.'

At Waterstones I asked, 'Can I buy every book you have about concussion, please?' They said, 'Knock yourself out.'

I was finally offered a job at Crufts but had to jump through hoops to get it.

I had a joke about a car with flat tyres – but it's going nowhere fast.

So it's your job to create coleslaw?
'Not full-time. It's just something I do on the side.'

Me: 'Doctor, I can't stop thinking about the
band Frankie Goes to Hollywood.'
Doctor: 'Relax.'

Want to see pictures of me driving diesel-fuelled
vehicles while wearing a variety of revealing
outfits? Subscribe to my OnlyVans page.

I saw five young men singing while bobbing
about in the sea – the latest buoy band.

Just before a lunchtime parachute jump,
a waiter came up and asked if he could
tempt me with another canopy.

Often I'll stroll languidly about my
house, collecting little packs of sugar.
I like to sachet around the place.

I saw a heavy goods vehicle with the words
'It was a pleasure to have been of some
assistance, however small' stencilled on
the side. It was an articulate lorry.

Sorry, I can't stop talking about aerial reconnaissance vehicles. Drone, drone, drone…

A boy at my school had top marks and perfect attendance records, despite being made of plastic. He was a model pupil.

I've started painting, using shots of coffee on canvas. It's good to espresso oneself.

I recommend putting a Victoria sponge in the oven. I like to have my cake and heat it.

I'm trying to write a joke about a penguin – but it just won't fly.

Horses can be so negative sometimes. Such neigh-sayers.

I need to do some online research about underwater eye protection. I'll goggle it.

I woke up, thinking that I owned a tobacconist's shop. Just a pipe dream.

My dad always takes a ladies' fan into the bookies. He enjoys a flutter.

I bought some cheese that was done up in tweed and wearing slippers – mature cheddar.

You can access real-time online footage of people's tears – streaming live.

After 24 hours trapped inside a lightbulb warehouse, I was ready to lamp someone.

I was late getting into the graffiti business. The writing was already on the wall.

Spider-Man got lots of high-end DIY equipment and then went on a training course on using them safely. With great power tools comes great responsibility.

My friends keep asking me, 'Where are we going? Weston-Super-Mare, Blackpool or Brighton?' I can't stand pier pressure.

I was sceptical at first about trying a skin treatment that involved putting ham on my face – but I was cured instantly.

A conjuror had too many props so he had to move them into the bedroom. That's where the magic happens.

My lawyer does try really hard – with the best will in the world.

My lawyer always used to sing 'With or Without You' and 'I Still Haven't Found What I'm Looking For' while working – Pro Bono.

Now my lawyer has asked to be paid in dog biscuits – Pro Bonio.

I was engrossed in a best-selling novel about sheet metal. Riveting stuff.

I tend to be quiet at the all-you-can-eat seafood buffet. I just clam up.

You'll never hear me boast about my love of hiring jazz instruments. I don't like to blow my own trumpet.

My great-grandad was a miner.
'Copper?'
No definitely a miner. The Police turned him down.

When counting, I have trouble with 1,3, 5, 7 and 9. I'm always against the odds.

When I started a job at the lion enclosure, they were biting my hand off to work with me.

Someone criticised me for complaining about having pins & needles. That touched a nerve.

It made good business sense to park my car between two stalls. There was a gap in the market.

A friend supplies cannons to historical re-enactments. Business is booming.

I saw a guy on a building site pushing a wheelbarrow full of roses, wine and chocolates – a labourer of love.

I hired a lazy personal trainer. He didn't work out.

So I hired a cowboy as a personal trainer. He spurred me into action.

Then I hired a dominatrix as a personal trainer. She soon whipped me into shape.

My nine-year-old niece goes around shouting, 'I'm the Firestarter, twisted Firestarter!' She's a child prodigy.

Someone asked me for directions to the new cannabis shop. I told him to try the High Street.

On arrival at a corporate event I was given a large package which contained Bill Oddie - who proceeded to tell me how well I was looking. It's always nice to get a complimentary Goodie bag.

I think someone has attacked my computer with a machete. Yes, my PC's definitely been hacked.

I consulted an archaeologist about cleaning my oven. I needed an expert in ancient grease.

*A mollusc wanted to get in touch
– but only by snail mail.*

A dictionary-compiler once told me to get lost. That's the very definition of rude.

*A librarian started an argument with
me – but I had no issues.*

Police were called to a disturbance at a 1970s theme-night at a Chinese restaurant. A witness said that 'Everybody was Kung Po fighting.'

On the motorway I avoided a collision with a lorry-load of razors. That was a close shave.

*I thought I did brilliantly when finding
out information about insects'
anatomy. I was the bees' knees.*

*I've used the same bathroom scales for
forty years. I'm set in my weighs.*

*The Chancellor of the Exchequer rode a motorbike
into Parliament – trying to kick-start the economy.*

*It's important that people take long
walks in the countryside in a sensible
manner. Please gambol responsibly.*

*My friend's daughter keeps saying, 'Leave me
alone, dad; Leave me alone, dad' over and
over. It's just a phrase she's going through.*

*I can't stop clicking my fingers. My
wife told me to snap out of it.*

*At an interview to work in the barbeque
section of my local garden centre,
they gave me a good grilling.*

*Then I went for a job driving a steamroller. At that
interview they went over my CV several times.*

I got the steamroller job and have been working flat-out ever since.

I love that vegetable whistle-blowing website – wiki-leeks.

I was disappointed when the restaurant flooded. I'd made a reservoiration.

Another restaurant was also flooded – after a damming review.

Genealogy became a hobby but I made a lot of mistakes. I kept barking up the wrong family tree.

The government commissioned a report into keeping secrets. The results were telling.

My password is always 'Snow White and the Seven Dwarves' – as it contains at least eight characters.

I had to force myself to go to the library in the rough area of town. I had some reservations.

I went to a nightclub full of bee-keepers. There was a real buzz in the room.

I got that new book all about glue.
I couldn't put it down.

There's a new play all about taxi-cabs.
Critics said it was hackneyed.

I want someone to benefit from my large keyboard
collection when I'm gone. I'm an organ donor.

I'm great at walking up an escalator
– took it to a whole new level.

My ex-partner was a civil engineer. We
eventually built some bridges between us.

I stored my photos on the cloud –
but they kept blowing away.

The worst job I had was as a tradesman on a
submarine. That was plumbing the depths.

The restaurant near me is so out of touch.
The soup of the day is primordial.

Grappling-hook chic? That'll never catch on.

I compiled a book of my selfies. Vanity publishing.

I saw a book all about storing wine
– this year's best cellar.

My wife recommends wine for skin care.
She always has a Rosé complexion.

That film about a famous guitarist – It
struck a chord with audiences.

Spiders are great with technology
– always on the web.

That tear-jerking movie about a jigsaw
puzzle? I was in pieces after it.

At boxing training, I mistook
my reflection for another fighter. I
tried not to beat myself up over it.

Then the same thing happened when I
switched to karate. I was kicking myself.

A falcon comes into church every
day – a bird of pray.

That book all about being single?
It'll end up on the shelf.

At a new play about wedding cakes,
the audience was in tiers.

People are protesting about using 90s tech
to communicate. They're Anti-Fax.

I keep a record of the amount of drawing pins I
use each year – for my annual tacks return.

Normally I don't do toilet humour but
this pun's pretty bog standard.

After the trouble with the drainage, no one
wanted to address the effluent in the room.

An internet influencer became a
postman. He delivered laterz.

After a disastrous toupee fitting, I was placed
into a medically-induced comb-over.

I took on a second-hand milliner's
business. It was old hat.

That new play about boxing – critics
described it as hard-hitting.

Frankenstein's Monster tried following Dracula
on Facebook but he un-fiended him.

Cards on the table: I keep making snap decisions.

I annoyed folk by turning up late to my knife-throwing club. People were giving me daggers.

As a manufacturer of roof tiles, I take it personally when my work is slated.

My book of Ancient Greek Philosophy was buried under some junk. I've had a lot on my Plato recently.

I'm all for poets' rights. Sometimes you have to make a stanza.

Obi Wan Kenobi was interrogated by two Welsh Stormtroopers. He convinced them that 'These aren't the druids you're looking for'.

A message flashed up on my computer screen, saying, 'Looking for a rod, line and tackle?' I can't stand phishing emails.

I was getting lots of emails about pork luncheon meat so now they go straight into my spam folder.

I saw that film about Oppenheimer. It bombed at the box office. And the critics said it was a dud.

I'm regularly photographed posing with bagels, buns and baps – a roll model.

I opened a cupboard and my watch collection fell on top of me. I've got lots of time on my hands.

I tried stir-frying some rainwater which blew into the kitchen during a gale – cooked up a storm.

They work you hard in the trouser-manufacturing plant. Wish my boss would cut me some slacks.

Although on the good days, my colleagues would have me in creases.

After some financial problems, though, the business was coming apart at the seams.

It's tough making food from nuts and berries – gruelling stuff.

I didn't do well in the 'hold your breath in the water' competition. I was bubbling under.

A reboot of 'How to Make an American Quilt'? It wouldn't be a patch on the original.

I see that LSD is getting 5-star reviews on Tripadvisor.

*On a Friday after work, I cover myself with
strawberry, apricot and cherry Bakewell.
It's nice to tart myself up for a night-out.*

*Government computers have been drenched
in gallons of Scrumpy. GCHQ are calling
it the worst cider-attack in history.*

*Cyclops needs to invest in more gadgets.
At the moment he only has one iPad.*

*I like to go into Currys and hug the brand
new laptops and mobiles. It's good to
embrace the latest technology.*

*Moses was at the forefront with
technology. He had two tablets.*

*People have called me a sponger. But I suppose
I am always on the lookout for free cake.*

*If you ever need assistance finding
out about Stephen King's scary clown
– try calling the IT Helpdesk.*

*Dave Grohl's band came down with tummy
bugs on tour and now there are Few Fighters.*

*After months of cajoling, a mate finally
returned Placido Domingo. That's
the last time I lend him a tenor.*

*The temperature was really
high when I was on holiday.
'In the nineties?'
No, just last week.*

*Lots of high-speed rodents were causing me
stress. I had to get out of the rat race.*

*I was looking at a couple of great websites all
about men's deodorant. I'll send you the lynx.*

*In the middle of a hurricane, I realised
I was desperate to charge my phone
– any USB port in a storm.*

*I laugh whenever I go into KFC
– Zingers every time.*

*Computer experts have set up a system of
listening to an ex-US Vice President doing
some drumming. It's an Al Gore-rhythm.*

*I wanted to catch up with my nudist
friend. He checked his diary and it
turns out he has nothing on.*

*When my boat got into trouble, I immediately
put on a pair of 1970s-style trousers.
Thank goodness for emergency flares.*

*The worst thing about being a member
of the Baggy Trousers Club? If I'm late
for a meeting, I always get pulled up.*

*I was nervous going for a job interview to work
at Coleman's – but I mustard up the courage.*

*I thought long and hard about buying
the 'Impossible-to-Understand
Joke Book'. I didn't get it.*

*I considered moving on from being an air traffic
controller – but a career change isn't on my radar.*

*My doctor has recommended Paint Therapy
– I must get in touch with my emulsions.*

*I saw some people scribbling things in
notebooks while walking backwards.
They were on a writing retreat.*

*I went to pick my friend's son up after
his lessons but brought home the
wrong child – schoolboy error.*

I decided to tell all about my time as a referee in GCHQ's staff football tournament. I'm a government whistle-blower.

We're going out for a burger and chips. 'Five Guys?' No, just the wife and I.

Have you heard about the quiz show host who is chased by ghosts in a maze? Jeremy Pac-Man.

Crime scene experts have been investigating a huge amount of desserts. The proof is in the pudding.

As well as being a wizard, Merlin was also good with herbs and spices – a legendary sauce-eror.

Historians have found evidence of mobile phones in the past – by re-examining the Charger of the Light Brigade.

At the Taxidermists' monthly get together for dinner, everyone was stuffed.

At the seal enclosure of the local aquarium, everyone enjoyed a slap-up meal.

I once walked in on a photo shoot for the band REM – that's me in the corner.

Judges in Liverpool are notoriously tough. They show no Mersey.

I'm part of a group which meets once a month to get emotionally overwrought about old objects. We're the local Hysterical Society.

I've joined a dating site for lumberjacks. Feel free to view my Timbrr profile.

Yes, officer. I saw Humpty Dumpty being kidnapped by two men. He was put in a car and whisked away.

Talking of Humpty Dumpty, our friendship is complicated. Feels like I'm constantly walking on eggshells around him.

My job interview to work in a fizzy drinks factory didn't go well. I bottled it.

I got that fizzy drinks job but was canned soon after.

I got into an argument about microwave ovens. Things got heated pretty quickly.

*My dad was furious with me for
borrowing his smoking jacket. He gave
me a proper dressing gown.*

*Remember that 1970s horror movie,
'Coma'? It was a sleeper hit.*

*That low-budget movie about fluffy
footwear? It was a slipper hit.*

*My chiropodist says my toes are nice and
will do me no harm – no mean feet.*

*Arranging as many bunches of flowers as
possible before I die – that's on my bouquet list.*

*I saw lots of zombies dancing all through the
night in a field – an all-night grave party.*

*I'm so lucky to play in a band with Professor
Brian Cox on keyboards – living the D:Ream.*

*I saw a film where cats took over a
ship – Mewtiny on the Bounty.*

*They once tried to drown a vampire in a vat of
stew – but Dracula has Risen from the Gravy.*

I took on a job as CEO of an elastics company.
To be honest, it was a bit of a stretch.

I now do two jobs for the price
of one - a promotion.

On a foggy night someone threw a whisky
bottle at me – but Scotch missed.

I like to give away paintings of snake-headed
Greek myths. I'm a Gorgon donor.

Remember that Sean Penn movie,
'Milk'? The critics lapped it up.

My hotcakes are selling like… erm,
I'll get back to you on that.

I'm determined to get people speaking French
in a polite manner. I'm on a merci mission.

I've heard of a group of local witches who
don't like cooking – a microwave coven.

There has been a large bang in a TV
news studio. Here's the report.

*Mr McPartlin thought of a system of
alphabetically listing his possessions while
at his partner's house – In Dec's.*

*Someone glued a pair of antique duelling
pistols to my hands. I'm sticking to my guns.*

*In restaurants I always give salt, pepper and
mustard to the cook. My condiments to the chef.*

*I makes lots of cups of tea without even
thinking about it. I brews very easily.*

*We still haven't come up with a suitable term
which describes the time it takes for planet Earth
to fully rotate once on its axis. Let's call it a day.*

*I've joined an elite unit of the police force which
specialises in keeping fit – the SQUAT team.*

*Stir-frying in an open green space?
That'll be a wok in the park.*

*I'm getting a new bearded, tattooed, skinny-
jeans-wearing young man – a hipster-
replacement operation on the NHS.*

*It can be depressing sitting in landfill sites. I
have been down in the dumps recently.*

I just walked past an 80s pop star.
I'm absolutely convinced.
'Adamant?'
No, Boy George.

Times were tough for Adam Ant during
lockdown. He had to Stand and Deliveroo.

I was always scared during science
lessons at school. I was petri-fied.

I love that old song that reminds me of Italian
restaurants – 'Take Another Little Pizza My Heart'.

The same goes for Indian restaurants –
'Take Another Little Pitta My Heart'.

It's a shame that Hercule Poirot got severe
tinnitus. He ended up Deaf on the Nile.

If you have tinnitus, then go and see my
GP. That's a ringing endorsement.

My doctor recommended that I go swimming with
dolphins. It was purely for medicinal porpoises.

Dire Straits always do well at Sotheby's.
They recently got a Monet for Nothing.

A farmer was concerned about his sheep grazing near a cliff. It was a shear drop.

The Prince of Wales has installed a new gym at Buckingham Palace. It's fit for a King.

Me: 'After brushing my teeth, I've been clenching my fists and swinging my arms around vigorously from the back and to the front.'
My dentist: 'I'm glad you've been flossing regularly.'

I've hired a tennis coach, costing a fortune. But I wasn't expecting to pay for a bus-load of people going to Wimbledon.

Blah blah blah, self-raising flour. Tumty-tum, three eggs. Yadda yadda yadda, freshly-grated zest…. That's my recipe for lemon drivel cake.

Fried egg, bacon, sausage, toast. This is the latest breakfast news.

I saw a bird in a tree which looked like a Hollywood star – the nest big thing.

The cleaner in my block of flats is going around with a scythe. I think it's the Grime Reaper.

I saw someone getting their picture taken alongside a sponge – selfie-absorbed.

I call the left and right sides of my brain 'tag-team' – as I'm always wrestling with my conscience.

My favourite snack is that brand of crisps created by monks – Monastery Munch.

Several footballers' girlfriends have formed their own occult coven. It's a real WAGs to Witches story.

Instead of taking his work seriously, my boss spends his days looking at pictures of 1970s cars. I'm tired of his Cavalier attitude.

Caught my wife talking on the phone in hushed tones about cod, halibut, haddock and salmon. Sounds a bit fishy to me.

Anyone wondering if my gravedigger job is full-time, I'm just filling in.

Why is the Titanic always crying? It's an emotional wreck.

The office has ventilation issues and the jamb must be repaired. But if you need to chat, my door is always open.

That meteor joke went right over my head.

I used to struggle with safe-cracking but then everything clicked into place.

*Although he's not the best cook, every January 25th my brother hosts an evening of traditional Scottish cuisine.
'Burns supper?'
Yes, he really should learn how to work the oven properly.*

*Went for a run with Connery, Lazenby, Moore, Dalton, Brosnan and Craig
– Good Bonding exercise.*

While driving towards the Humber, there were dozens of prototype adult toys strewn along the streets. The road to Hull is paved with rude inventions.

I was being emailed so many pictures of 12th Century Chinese sailing ships that they now go straight into my junk folder.

I enjoy going to rap battles with young goats. I'm down with the kids.

Saw some people coming out of church with congealed potato on their foreheads. Must be Mash Wednesday.

I've lost 2000 raisins, 1000 sultanas and 500 dried grapes. Fraudsters emptied my currant account.

Yes, I do know Trigger, Compo, Father Dougal and Norman Wisdom – Fool disclosure.

My toddler nephew is feeling guilty about making a mess with alphabetti spaghetti. It's written all over his face.

There have been complaints that I have too many books. Even my shelves are groaning.

You will also enjoy...

Printed in Great Britain
by Amazon

23492894R00037